Who Is Taller?

words by Amanda Graham
photographs by Lisa James

Dad is tall. He is much taller than I am. He can get the ball out of the tree. I can't.

Who is shorter?

I am much shorter than Dad is.

I can go into the tunnel. He can't.

Who is heavier?

Dad is much heavier than I am. He can hold the seesaw on the ground. I can't.

Who is lighter?

7

8

I am much lighter than Dad is.

I can sit on Dad's shoulders.

He can't sit on mine.

Who can go higher?

Dad can go much higher than I can. He can swing up to the sky. I can't.

Who can go lower?

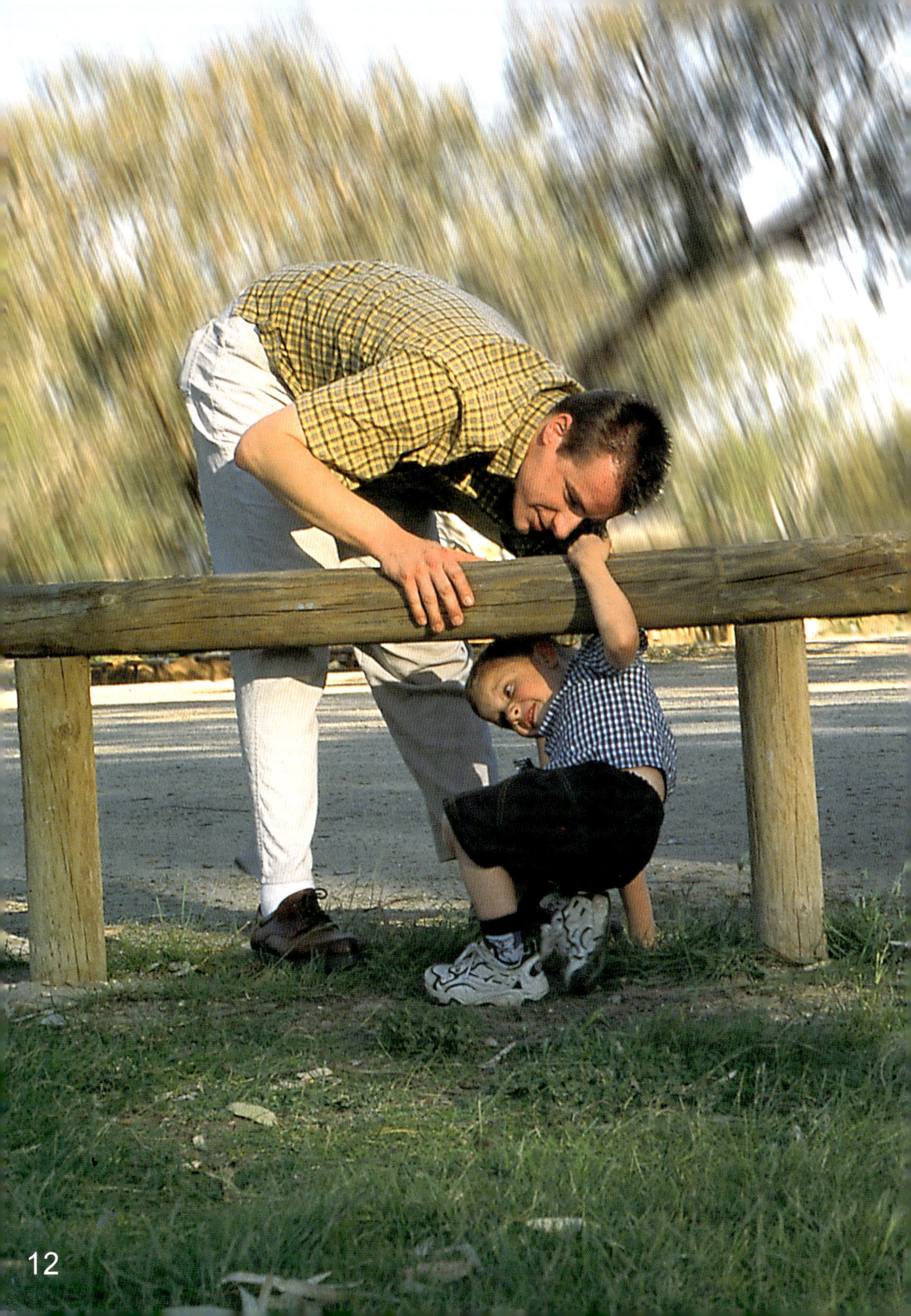

I can go much lower than Dad can. I can go under the bar. He can't.

Who is faster?

Dad is much faster than I am.

He can win the race to the gate.

I can't.

Who is slower?

I am much slower than Dad is.
I have lots of ice cream left.
He has none. Poor Dad.